For DAD, who always
supported and inspired me,
and who shared with me
his knowledGe of the universe,
his wit, and his lauGhter.

WeiRd is Normal When TeenaGers GRIEVE

Jenny Lee Wheeler

Quality
of Life
Publishing Co.

© 2010
by Jenny Lee Wheeler

Second Printing 2013

Published by:

P.O. Box 112050
Naples, Florida 34108-1929

Toll Free: 1 (877) 513-0099 (in U.S. and Canada)
Phone: (239) 513-9907
Fax: (239) 513-0088

www.QoLpublishing.com

Quality of Life Publishing Co. is an independent publisher
specializing in heartfelt gentle grief support, as well as
books that educate, inspire, and motivate.

*Front cover design by Jenny Lee Wheeler and Kelly Brachle,
inspired by software at www.wordle.net.*

**ISBN 13: 978-0-9816219-8-2
ISBN 10: 0-9816219-8-8**

Library of Congress Control Number: 2010910591

CoNtents

ForewoRd

By Dr. Heidi Horsley

teen grief is often overlooked and unacknowledged because teenagers tend to value privacy regarding their feelings. When you do share your thoughts and feelings, it is often with friends. That is what makes this book a particularly interesting read, as 16-year-old Jenny Wheeler openly shares her personal experience of loss following the death of her father to cancer. It is truly an inspiration that Jenny would have the discipline to chronicle her journey and share her insights for the benefit of you and others.

I, myself, was only 20, just out of my teens, when my 17-year-old brother Scott and cousin Matthew were killed in an automobile accident. Like Jenny, I know and have lived the pain of family loss.

When you are growing up, you just assume that your parents and siblings won't die until you are well into your adult years. Death of a sibling or death of a parent, while you are still in your teens, is not something you expect or that you are prepared for. It feels out of order, turns your world upside down, and just feels wrong. But as this book shows us, teens do have these experiences, and Jenny shares with us her story of not only surviving a loss, but also finding hope again.

Since 2002 I have worked on the Columbia University Family Guidance Program with teens who lost firefighter fathers in the World Trade Center tragedy. I have watched them display a range of emotions, including resentment and anger, following the enormous loss of their fathers. I have also seen these same teens laugh and cry as we talk about all their memories of and love for their dads.

Ambivalence is part of the teenage experience. Friends mean well but want to see you get back to normal. Adults might think you aren't grieving when you don't feel like talking to them about your loss and instead you do things like attend parties, play video games, or find a game of basketball. But you *are* grieving, just in your own way and on your own time.

My sister Heather, who was 14 at the time of our brother Scott's death, wore headphones and listened to Grateful Dead music for years. As an adult, she tells us that it was not because she wasn't grieving but because she found the music soothing and an escape from her painful feelings of loss.

Jenny's journey, I believe, will strike a note with teenagers everywhere who have experienced the loss of someone they love. She gives sound advice and lets you know you are not alone. As this book shows, as teens, you often express your grief in creative ways, such as through art, music, journaling, and blogging.

Jenny has given us a remarkable look through her window of personal experience of early father loss. Her memories of her dad spending time in his home office are compelling. Her story and advice to others are heart-rending and real, with a gentle longing for the life she once had and the realization that life will never be the same. However, she also leaves us with the message that there is hope after loss. Although our losses may define us, they will not destroy us. As Jenny, the 9/11 teens, and my sisters and I know, love goes on and can never break the bonds with those we have loved and lost.

To surviving parents, friends, and family: This book is a valuable resource, and it will help you to get into the heads and hearts of bereaved adolescents. Jenny's story also lends itself to a possibility of dialogue. I would suggest saying to your teen: "I picked up this book today written by a grieving teen, and I was wondering what you might think about her experience." It would also be an excellent book to use as a reference for adolescent bereavement groups.

Also, I would be remiss if I did not comment on the strength and courage of the surviving parents. As with the amazing 9/11 firefighter widows, Jenny's mom Karla Wheeler deserves huge credit for encouraging Jenny in this project. Jenny and Karla show us that out of loss can come creativity, hope, and healing that can truly impact the world and ease the burden of grieving adolescents everywhere. I would also like to pay tribute to my own mother, Gloria Horsley, who started the online grief support community Open to Hope in honor of my brother Scott. Although those we have loved and lost are gone, they will live forever in our hearts and in our memories.

— *Dr. Heidi Horsley, New York City*
Adjunct Professor of Columbia University School of Social Work and co-author of
Teen Grief Relief: Parenting with Understanding, Support, and Guidance

PART I: GRIEVING *is* Normal

IntRoduction

Dr. Heidi Horsley, who wrote the Foreword for this book and has helped teenagers who lost their firefighter fathers in the 9/11 tragedy, tells me grieving is normal, that grief and life often go hand in hand. I have found that it is perfectly normal to be grieving if you have lost someone close to you. But you may ask how I can accurately tell you that grieving is normal when the title of this book clearly says that, for teenagers, grieving is weird. This is because when I use the word "normal," in this case I mean "supposed to happen." If you are grieving, nothing is wrong with you, even if you feel you are grieving in different ways than adults (which is where the "weird" comes in). In fact, if someone you love has died and you aren't grieving, I'd suggest you read this book (which apparently you already are!).

Chapter 1

My Path of GRIEF

hroughout my life I have experienced grieving a number of different times. I guess you could say I am fairly "experienced" with grief because I know how it feels, at various ages, to have someone you love die. The first time I lost someone close to me was when I was 5 years old. Both of my grandfathers died a few weeks apart, and I missed them a lot.

I loved both of them and enjoyed spending time with them. My "Grampa Dutch," my mom's dad, lived near us and would come over to our house some mornings. I remember how he would always greet me with a huge hug, and then we'd devour together a treat he brought, like donut holes. When we would travel to Canada to see Grandpa Wheeler, my dad's dad, we would play games. He taught me how to wink, and we would see who could wink alternating eyes the fastest. I really missed playing games with him.

Luckily, my mom was a local volunteer grief counselor, and she told me it was okay to share any feelings that I had, happy or sad. She encouraged my dad and me to express how sad or happy we were, and what we were thinking about the grandpas.

When I was 11, my "Gramma Ree Ree," what I called my mom's mother, died after being sick with lung cancer for about a year. Because she lived nearby, sometimes I helped my mom take care of her because Grampa Dutch had died a few years earlier and she lived by herself. My grandma and I had been very close. Ever since I was little she would babysit me when both of my parents were working. We would play with her cats together and make up fun games. One of my favorites involved tossing a cat toy, trying to land it in a certain spot on the floor. When I would miss she would re-peat, "Close, but no cigar." I was sad when she died, but it helped that our family already knew how to talk about our feelings and give each other support.

The most recent — and most painful — death in my family happened when I was 14, about a year and a half before I had the idea to write this book. My dad, who had always been healthy, was diagnosed with a type of cancer called lymphoma. He entered the hospital and underwent several chemotherapy sessions, but he died about a month later. It was painful to watch him get sicker. One day

I wouldn't have known there was anything wrong, and the next day I had to think about the idea that he might be really sick.

At breakfast each morning, Dad and I would eat cereal and read the comics page of the newspaper. Many evenings, we'd watch an episode of *Star Trek* or *Mythbusters* before I started my homework. Within a few weeks, all my time with Dad was spent in a hospital room when I would visit him every day after school.

I would try to squeeze our usual amount of visiting into a few hours so I could do my homework, and I would describe to him everything that had happened that day at school. Gradually he wasn't feeling like his normal self, and he would be tired or irritable. It was hard for me to see him get frustrated about little things that wouldn't have bothered him if he had been feeling better. His cancer spread quickly throughout his body, so his little hospital room was exchanged for a portion of the crowded Intensive Care Unit, sectioned off by a curtain. At this point only a breathing machine kept him alive. He could no longer talk, and the pain medicine made him sleep most all the time. We knew then he was dying.

I remember the day my mom told me that we were going to honor Dad's wishes and remove him from the life-support machines. Years earlier he had signed a Living Will stating that he would not like to be kept alive by life support if he was that sick. My mom,

Grandma Wheeler from Canada, and a few other close family members all gathered around Dad's hospital bed that Sunday afternoon as he was dying. We kept telling Dad how much we loved him, and I was thanking him over and over again for being such a great dad to me. Even though it was strange to think that within a few minutes he would no longer be alive, we were able to tell him that we would be okay and that he could go in peace. As he died right in front of us, I felt relieved that he was no longer suffering but sad that beginning at that moment my own dad was no longer alive. I felt like I crossed over some sort of barrier, like I was automatically in a new part of my life — the part after my dad died.

That day felt very strange to me, and when we got home from the hospital I sat alone and dangled my feet into the pool while my mom talked with our relatives. It felt like I was taking a breather, sitting and thinking for maybe 15 minutes. When my mom came and told me I had been sitting there for about 45 minutes, I couldn't believe it.

Although I was in a pretty good place about Dad's death, I began to miss him a lot. He had been, for me, the best dad ever, always interested in whatever I was doing. He had a scientific mind and would teach me things about the universe starting at a young age. He had a great sense of humor, and we would often laugh hysterically about something he said or some "inside" joke. He made me laugh with his wacky sense of humor. Since I'm an only child, Dad found it easy to make room in his busy schedule to spend lots of time with me.

My mom and I cried together often after Dad died and shared/compared how we were both feeling. Letting all those emotions out helped me grieve. Today, I'm less sad about Dad's death, but I still miss him and like to talk about him.

After my dad died, I began to notice that I grieved differently from the adults around me. For instance, when my dad's birthday rolled around, the adults in the room were sad, and some were even crying. But I didn't feel sad just because it was Dad's birthday and he wasn't here. Instead, I felt like smiling as I remembered how he liked to sing his own version of "Happy Birthday" to himself. He'd change the words and sing, "Hippo birdie to me, hippo birdie to me, hippo birdie, dear Gerry, hippo birdie to me."

Sometimes the opposite happened, and I'd be the only one sad or crying. No one else around me who knew and loved Dad would be showing any signs of grief, but I'd have a grief attack that was triggered by something that would probably seem bizarre to the average grownup. To me, a grief attack happens when an unexpected wave of grief comes crashing down upon me. In the second part of the book where I talk about how grieving is weird, you'll read that my grief attacks were sparked by weird things like the closing of a local amusement park, a microwave oven that stopped working, and trying to decide whether or not to polish my toenails as I got ready to go to a friend's fancy party.

As I noticed more and more of these differences between the ways adults and teenagers grieved, I told my mom I wanted teenagers to know that they aren't going crazy if their grief attacks seem weird. I also wanted teenagers to know they aren't going crazy if they see signs of continued love from their loved one (you'll read all about signs in Part IV). Because my mom is the founder of Quality of Life Publishing, which publishes grief support books, she encouraged me to write this book.

As you're reading these pages, please don't think of me as an "expert," someone who knows everything about this subject. Also, you don't have to agree with everything I say. I'm just sharing my experiences as I understand them.

Writing this book really helped me to heal from some of the grief I have about my dad's death, and I hope that what I have written helps you to know that there are others out there — especially other teenagers — who understand what you are going through and want to encourage you to be open to the hope of healing from your loss.

At a GLance:

• *Grieving has been a normal part of my life ever since I was 5 years old when my grandfathers died weeks apart.*

• *As a family, we found ways to talk about our sadness and express our feelings of loss. This helped me after my grandma died when I was 11, and especially after my dad died three years later.*

• *Dad's death left a huge hole in my life, and I cried a lot.*

• *I noticed I grieved differently from the adults around me, which is one reason I wrote this book. I want other teenagers to know this is normal!*

• *Writing this book helped me to heal, and I hope it helps you know that grieving is normal, you're not alone, and there is hope that you will heal, too.*

Chapter 2

EveRybody GRIEVES

the first thing I'd like to do is give you permission to grieve. You have the right to be grieving, whether you have lost a friend, family member, or even a pet. No type of loss is too small. One person could lose their grandparent and another lose their dog, and both people would have the right to be grieving and to receive support from others. Also, you don't have to get over your loss according to any certain timetable; you always have the right to grieve and to need comfort from others. And you don't need to act tough or unaffected by the loss to show other people that you are strong.

Nobody can tell you that you shouldn't grieve over a certain loss. As Dr. Heidi wrote in the beginning of this book, she lost her brother Scott in an auto accident when she was just out of her teens and away at college. She was very sad to have lost such a close family member, and it would really bug her when people would ask her how her parents were doing, as if the death of her brother affected only her parents and not her and her younger sisters. Heidi told me it felt like she and her sisters had no right to grieve.

A few years ago, I lost my best-friend cat, George, whom I had grown up with. George was like my shadow; he loved to follow me around the house and sleep curled up next to me every night. Losing him felt just like losing a family member. Kids at the summer camp I was attending at my friend Hannah's house sent me sympathy cards after George died, and when I didn't show up to certain events, they knew it was because I was sad and not in a party mood. Every loss is a valid one. Even the loss of a pet can be hard.

You never need to be embarrassed about the fact that you are grieving, even if it has been a long time since you have lost that person or pet. The fact is, many people continue to grieve the loss of a loved one even if the loss happened years and years ago. Our society tends to pressure those who are grieving to "get over it" or "snap out of it." Everyone grieves differently and in his or her own time depending on the individual person, the kind of loss he or she experienced, and the rate at which the grieving person gets in touch with his or her emotions.

At a GLance:

- *You have the right to be grieving no matter what; no loss is too small.*

- *You don't have to act tough to show others how strong you are.*

- *You don't need to be embarrassed about grieving.*

- *You don't have to grieve according to someone else's timetable.*

- *You don't have to "get over" your loss or "snap out of it" because of someone else's expectations.*

- *We all grieve in our own way and in our own time.*

Chapter 3

Share Your FeelinGs;
Show Your GRIEF

You don't have to "suck it up" to look strong for your friends or family. Even if you are acting as a role model for younger siblings or friends, it's always better to let your grief show. You will be more of a role model by showing them that it's okay to be sad when you feel hurt. Hiding your feelings or tears and closing yourself off to other people won't make you stronger or more responsible; it will only hurt you more in the long run.

When you are grieving a loss, keeping your feelings hidden deep inside isn't the best way to deal with it. Some people might try to hide their feelings to seem strong or "shelter" family members from their emotions, but this really isn't the best approach. No matter how hard it might seem, it is important to share your feelings rather than keep them hidden inside where no one can see them and help

---

you with them.

If you feel like you need support, open up to someone you can trust. Maybe it's a friend, a teacher or counselor at school, the mom or dad of a close friend, a minister at church, the coach of your sports team, or a neighbor. If you feel like you're not understood as well as you'd like, you can at least tell your family and friends that you are sad because you miss your loved person or pet. Not everyone will know what to say, but the people who care about you will do their best to support you and comfort you in any way they can, even if it's just giving you a hug or listening to you when you talk.

If you tell friends and family you trust that you are grieving, they will probably understand and react by giving you the extra support you need. If some of your friends don't understand or accept how you feel, it may be because they don't know what to say. They may feel uncomfortable because they don't know what you're thinking or what to do. Don't let this hurt your feelings, because talking about grief doesn't come naturally to everyone.

When my dad went into the hospital, some friends at school would comfort me and some wouldn't say anything. One friend at first said nothing, then one day asked shyly, "Is it okay if I ask how your dad is?" So even though I say that telling friends and family you are grieving or feeling sad is a good thing, don't take it personally if some people don't feel comfortable talking about grief.

If it's a family loss, your family members will probably be feeling the same way, and telling them when you're sad will let them know that they can share their feelings as well. *Everyone* is allowed to grieve. You don't have to act tough for fear your friends won't understand or will think you are a "baby." No one will think you are immature if they know you are going through a rough time.

When I went back to school after my dad's memorial service, pretty much all the teachers and most of my classmates asked how my mom and I were doing and if there was anything they could do to help us. Several of my classmates' mothers did favors for us, helping us around the house, making us dinner, picking me up from school, and helping with other things that my dad was no longer there to do. Neighbors and friends also supported us, and several of my dad's friends offered to help us with mechanical or computer-related tasks that my dad would have done. Because my dad was both a technical whiz and a packrat, there were many times when my mom or I would stumble across some old-looking piece of hardware and think, *What the heck is this and what does it do?* Having my dad's friends come and sort junk for us really helped.

Each time someone did us a favor like this, my mom and I would let them know that it really meant a lot to us. We needed people to reach out to so that we wouldn't become stuck, alone in the painful pit of grief many people think you have to stay in. People probably wouldn't have taken those extra steps to help us if we hadn't let them know how we felt. You could say we were reaching over the side of the pit sending out SOS signals, rather than just thinking we'd have to deal with our loss alone.

SuppoRt GRoups Can Help

After my grandpas died, I joined my school's grief support group the next fall, and it was a great way to share my feelings. It was a place where I could be around other grieving people my age (I was about 6 at the time). It was pretty much the only place I've been where you could walk up to someone you don't know and say, "Who do you miss who died? I'm here because of my grandpas," and not get weird looks or make someone else start crying. We went around the room at the beginning of the camp and talked about who we were missing who had died. Some kids had lost a dog, a few had lost a parent, and I clearly had the longest list, because I insisted on adding not only both of my grandpas, but also the six or seven short-lived goldfish I had as pets within the last year or two.

We all got packets that had tips for grieving or remembering our loved ones, but my favorite part was coloring the packet with brightly colored markers after we had finished a page. Not all kids liked the same activity, but we all seemed to have fun in some way. Support groups like this one are common, and they help many people. The one at my school was run by our local hospice. Maybe you will find such a group at your school or church. However, you don't have to join a support group to talk to other people about your grief, or to help others with their grief.

It's healthy to find people who have experienced similar losses who can share their own stories and feelings with you, and vice versa. Whether you find them at a support group, in school, or anywhere else, it's good to know that you're not alone in your grief. Try asking around — someone you know could be grieving or have gone through grief before, even if you didn't know them at the time.

OtheR Ways to Express FeelinGs

Throughout this book, I mention talking as a way to express your grief because I have been fortunate enough to be around friends and family who are pretty supportive. However, I know that not everyone is in this situation. Expressing feelings through conversation is not the most comfortable to everyone, and certain people might feel like they have no one to talk to. Talking things out is a really great way of working through grief, but it is only one method, and not everyone has to do it exactly as I've described here. However, I would be willing to bet that most everyone has at least one other person he or she can talk to about these things. One person to talk to is really all you need.

If you don't think talking it out is the best way for you (and please don't think you're not doing it right if you choose *not* to talk about your grief), there are many other ways of expressing your emotions. Activities like writing (keeping a journal of your feelings, writing poems or letters to your loved one), art (drawing, painting, sculpting), music (listening, singing, playing an instrument, composing your own lyrics and melodies), and other healthy activities that come naturally to you are also good ways to express some of the emotions you are feeling.

Inviting your friends to tune into your feelings through updates you provide on Facebook, blogs, or other online networking sites might be another outlet for you. I didn't belong to Facebook when my dad died. But now that I'm active on Facebook, I can see how it would be a great connecting tool for grieving teens. Maybe you'd want to write that you're feeling sad and give your friends a chance to show they care. I'm sure there are tons of things you can do on Facebook and other sites that reflect how you're feeling on any given day.

At a GLance:

- *If you're a role model for younger kids, let your grief show instead of sheltering family members from your tears.*

- *It is important to share your feelings; "sucking it up" will only hurt you more.*

- *Reach out to others, and most of them will try to reach back.*

- *Support groups might be helpful.*

- *People with similar experiences can help you, give you advice, or simply listen to you.*

- *If you find it's too hard to talk about your grief, that's okay! Maybe you can express your feelings in other healthy ways, like through writing, art, music, or other activities unique to you.*

- *Facebook or other online networking sites offer ways to let others know how you're feeling.*

Chapter 4

Your FeelinGs Are YOUR FeelinGs

a good way to help sort out your feelings and deal with your grief is to realize that what you feel is what *you* feel, and it is not necessarily what he, she, they, or anyone else feels. Because everyone grieves and mourns differently, no one can tell you how you should or shouldn't feel. Some people might expect you to be over your grief sooner than you're ready to be. Others might assume they know how you feel when they really don't.

When people don't know how to approach a touchy subject like death, they'll often try to find some way to tell you that they're thinking about you. They may say something like, "I'm sorry. You must feel so awful," but you don't have to agree with them. If someone is telling you that you are feeling something you are not, you shouldn't think, "I must have to feel that way because they are telling me that, and I am in no state of mind to think for myself right now."

The truth is that even though you have experienced a loss — whether recently or not — that doesn't mean you are "out of it" or need coaching on how you should feel. Even though you may feel fragile because you're going through a rough time, you still know your feelings better than anyone else does, and all of your feelings are still real to you. If you seek guidance by joining a support group or talking to a friend, family member, teacher, or someone else close to you, this can help you sort out your feelings and understand why you are feeling how you are. This allows you to heal your emotions in your own way, instead of having someone else tell you how to feel.

I find that some people tend to over-exaggerate or under-exaggerate the grief of teenagers. This is done mostly by adults, but sometimes other teenagers misjudge this as well. Soon after my dad died I found that people seemed to pressure me in two main ways. One was to "get over it." Some people seem to think that it is normal to get over your loss within a short period of time. When your grieving takes longer, they might think you are too emotional and need to "snap out of it."

The other way I felt pressure — and maybe you do, too — was when someone said, "I feel so bad for you," or "You must be so upset." If you're not feeling sad at that moment, you might feel like you should be sad and down.

These ways of thinking are mindsets that you don't need to be pressured into. People sometimes have preset ideas that you should either mope around or get right back to your daily routine, but that is not necessarily what you're supposed to do. Remember that you are grieving on your own personal timetable, no one else's.

'Get Over It!' (The PressuRes to Hide Emotions)

"It's been a year already! Aren't you over it by now?"

"Suck it up!"

"Face reality. He's gone. Get on with your life!"

If you are hearing any of these things from anybody, take it with a grain of salt, or a whole *jar* of salt! Don't pay attention to questions or commands like these. Such statements can cause us to push all of our feelings inside in order to act more mature, or what we *think* is more mature. No one should have to do this, but especially teenagers because we are still growing emotionally and *need* to share our feelings. Grief has to be dealt with eventually, so if you scrunch all your feelings on the inside when the grief is still fresh, the feelings will come back later and be harder to deal with. Talk about your grief, or express it in some other safe way, and surround yourself with people who understand that this is still a really sensitive time for you.

While talking to a group of friends during the holidays, I commented about my dad. One friend said something like, "Oh! It's been a year already, hasn't it? You're still grieving?" This was obviously somebody who hadn't had any experience with loss. Instead of getting upset, I simply explained to her that, yes, I was still in the process of healing from my grief, and I still needed support from friends and family. My friend seemed surprised. You might find that not everyone will be as sensitive to your feelings as you would like them to be. Try not to take it personally.

If you are confronted by someone who thinks that you should be over your grief, hang tough. I try to either ignore the comment or simply explain that I am still grieving and not over my loss yet. If you are around people you can trust to support you and respect your feelings, you may want to say that talking and sharing would help you, that you still need support and people to talk with about your grief. If that person wants to understand your feelings, he or she might respond by asking you about how you are feeling more often, instead of just assuming how you feel.

I have found that some people are great at *really talking* about things with you and tuning into your feelings, but this kind of conversation does not come easily to everyone. Some people feel awkward talking about death and don't know what to say to someone who is grieving. You might even find that some people you thought were your friends start to avoid you. Again, don't take it personally. It's just that they don't know what to say or do around someone like you who is grieving. While these friends might fade into the background at times, other acquaintances who *are* comfortable reaching out to you might come into your life and become new friends.

The first special occasion after losing a loved one is tough — such as a birthday, Mother's Day, Father's Day, or holiday season — and it might even be a horrible nightmare for some people. However, I find that on the second occasion, and the ones after, most people forget you have lost somebody special. After the protective bubble of numbness has gone away, you're left to face the reality of grief, and that is often tough or even tougher to get through. I feel as if the "first" holidays are like the first stages of Pacman after your player has been gobbled up. He comes back, blinking on and off to tell you that he can walk around a little bit, eating the little bits of yellow on your screen, and he can do anything. He has been faced with death, so now he can walk through ghosts and still survive. This period of "blinking" time is what I consider to be a bubble of numbness. The first year or so of grief, many people gave me sympathies or hugged me, and I kind of walked around saying "Thank you," "It's okay," and other things, so numb that getting through the day wasn't actually that hard. I couldn't forget for a moment that people cared about my grief, which helped as well. However, soon Pacman gains strength and doesn't need the blinking protection. He can be eaten, now, so he needs to be careful again. The second Christmas and on other significant calendar dates since my dad died, it was almost as if I were shocked that we were having yet another holiday season or special occasion without Dad.

Of course, I had always known that the routines and traditions of people's lives would not end just because my dad died. The first year I was so focused on getting through "just this one," like running one more lap in a race, that I didn't even think about the next one. Thus, by the time I was there, I felt dumbfounded, like I was thinking, *Okay, so I've already done this. I've already had a Christmas since Dad died, and I did it. But now it's Christmas again, and he's still not back.* It was like I was realizing that, unlike the routine times of year, my Dad didn't go back to normal — or back to life — after one experience with Christmas. The second one is like the first time you realize your loved one isn't going to come back to life, exactly the way he or she was. It's going to stay this way. It wasn't as if I only had to face one Christmas without Dad, and then everything would be as it had been before.

This past Christmas, the second since I lost my dad, not as many people asked about my dad or how we were doing. In fact, the topic hardly came up at Christmastime this year. There were some people who hugged me and asked me how I was doing, because they knew that the second holiday season after your loved one dies is often no easier than the first. Most people didn't say anything, however, but I knew not to take their silence personally.

People will be more likely to understand you if you tell them you need more time to deal with your grief, even if you are not sad as often as you used to be when it was fresh. I am happier most of the time now, and my mom and I have become accustomed to our lives together without Dad by our side. Even so, every once in a while I'll come face-to-face with a grief attack and cry (I explain grief attacks in Chapter 5). I think about my dad every day, but especially around holidays like Christmas, Father's Day, and our birthdays, because my dad can't physically be around for them any-more. It's normal to experience grief around dates that were impor-tant to you and your loved one — even years after your loved one died.

It helps me to know that I don't have to follow a timetable for healing my grief and that I can't get over it *just like that* without healing from the inside. Everyone who mourns needs to heal their grief from the inside out by recognizing their emotions, in their own way and in their own time. It is okay if your healing takes a while; it also depends on what kind of loss you have had. Losing my dad might take me longer to grieve than someone else who lost their grandparent, but maybe not! Dr. Heidi and other grief counselors say the length of time someone feels like they are actively grieving depends on the individual, how sudden the death was, and how much support that person gets from others.

Unexpected losses may also be harder to deal with. When my cat died, I actually grieved for almost as long as I have for my dad. With my dad, I got to see him in the hospital for a while, but my cat was perfectly healthy until he died rather suddenly of kidney failure, and I only had one day to cope with his being sick before he died.

'I Feel So Bad for You!' (The PressuRes of OtheRs Telling You How You Should Feel)

When my dad died, I found from the way many people shared their sympathy with me that I often didn't feel as sad as they thought I did. It may have been a little easier for me, because I believe he is still with me, always, in spirit. Feeling that he is still with me helps me cope with my grief. Maybe this would help you, too. Also, I got to see him often when he was sick and had time to get used to the idea he would not survive his illness. I found that after my dad died, especially when it was fairly recent, people would approach the topic by saying things like, "I'm sorry about your dad. You must be really sad," when that wasn't exactly the way I was feeling at the time. Everybody's situation is different.

What I have found since my dad died is that when people aren't sure exactly what to say, they'll say things like, "I feel so bad for you!" or "I don't even know how you get out of bed in the morning!" It is okay that people say these things, as long as you don't let them get you down. If you *are* feeling this way, then it's great that these people are talking to you about your feelings, and it always feels good when someone tunes in to how *you* feel.

However, if you don't feel this way, you can just say, "Thank you," "That's okay," or something else that acknowledges their statement but allows you to change the subject if you feel the need. If this is someone you can talk to comfortably, explain to him or her that these aren't the feelings you are having. It's like the opposite of my holiday-time situation. Let them know that you are at a stage where you are happier so this person will know where you are emotionally when they talk to you in the future.

Some people would talk to me months after my dad died and say things like, "You poor thing," or "What a major blow to have your dad die like that," but, at that point, I wasn't thinking that at all and didn't want to feel pitied. Sometimes I thought, "Dad is with us always, just not here on this planet." Or when my mom and I started giving talks about grief and healing, sometimes travelling across the country, I would think, "This is great that my mom and I now get to talk to people about grief together," and "I might write a book about this to help other teenagers!"

What other people would say to me didn't always resonate with me, or, in other words, it wasn't necessarily true to me personally. This is when it's okay to nod, smile, and say, "Thank you" if you are not feeling the same way that person thinks you are. Remember that you don't have to feel sad just because someone thinks you should feel sad, just like you don't have to be over your grief when someone thinks you should be over it.

Whether you are feeling upset, sad, happy, frustrated, hopeful, numb, positive, angry, or anything else, no feeling is the wrong feeling. You have the right to feel however you feel, and whatever you feel is okay. Sometimes teenagers get lost in the shuffle when it comes to grief, because we are expected to control our emotions more than little kids do but often don't get the chance to share our feelings the way adults do. As teenagers, we tend to share our feelings in short bursts, especially when we have the free time to do so. Unlike some adults who can take a leave of absence from their jobs, we can't just stop going to school or take more than a few days off after a family member dies. We have to fit our grieving into our own time. I think it's important to recognize that, in a way, we *are* able to control ourselves and deal with our feelings better than young children, but we are not completely grown up yet, especially emotionally.

At a GLance:

- *Your feelings, no matter what they are, are always valid, even when you are grieving.*

- *No one can tell you how you should feel; ignore comments that you do not agree with or that don't reflect how you really feel.*

- *As teens, we are still growing emotionally and need to share our feelings — especially feelings of grief.*

- *Don't take it personally if some people — even some of your friends — don't know what to say to you and start to avoid you. Many people feel awkward talking about death.*

- *The first holiday, birthday, and other special dates after your loved one has died are difficult, but sometimes the second one can be even harder!*

- *It's okay if healing from your loss takes a long time.*

- *It's normal for people to say awkward things to you. Just don't let them pressure you to feel the way they think you should feel.*

• *No feeling is the wrong feeling. You have the right to feel whatever you are feeling.*

• *Sometimes grieving teens get lost in the shuffle; we're expected to be more in control than children, but we don't often get the chance to share our feelings the way adults do.*

PART II:
GRIEVING is WeiRd

IntRoduction

For us as teenagers, thoughts that seem weird are the norm. You might find yourself thinking, "Am I the only one who does this?" or "Do other people my age feel this way?" Grief experts say the answer is yes; other teenagers act similarly when dealing with similar events or challenges, even if the "similar" part is that we're all different. For teenagers, grieving is weird because it is different for each one of us, and it is especially different from adults' grief.

If you hear other teenagers' stories, you will find that most of our grief can be bizarre and come in many different forms. As a teenager, I know I'm unpredictable, with my moods changing often at times. Since we're not yet adults, we're not expected to behave like adults, which is good. This means we can grieve in our own ways, which can often be more effective than grieving in the standard "adult way." I think that through our own unique expressions we can get our feelings out more easily, and sometimes more honestly, than adults do.

Chapter 5

GRIEF Attacks:
EveRybody Has Them

grief attacks don't always come when you expect them to. What I mean by a "grief attack" is a time when an unexpected wave of grief comes crashing down upon us. Some things that you would expect to trigger a grief attack — like seeing someone who looks just like your loved one — might not trigger one at all. On the other hand, there could be a special trigger in your mind that suddenly makes you overcome with grief, even if you don't know why at first. I find that grief attacks can be very unpredictable.

Sometimes when a grief attack hits, you might feel trapped in a situation, afraid to show your emotions. But you don't need to hold back tears and hide your emotions from other people. If you let the people you are with know that some thought or event suddenly made you feel the emptiness of not having your loved one around, hopefully they will comfort you, not tease you! Again, it is important to know that tears aren't a sign of weakness. Tears help us let out the pain of what we're feeling; they aren't a meter showing how emotionally strong we are.

When my dad died, I shed a lot of tears and cried myself to sleep some nights. I still do this every once in a while. But when someone mentions my dad or when I experience a daily reminder of him, like seeing a picture or hearing a song he liked, sometimes I don't feel sad at all. Because many people would think such an obvious reminder should automatically make me feel sad, I used to feel guilty that I wasn't crying, especially when Dad's death was still recent. As I mentioned in a previous chapter, you don't need to feel bad if you don't feel sad when someone thinks you should. Not only do teenagers and adults grieve differently, but teenagers also grieve differently from *each other,* so you shouldn't feel like you're supposed to react to a particular comment or event the way I do or any other teen does.

Sometimes things happen the other way around. Someone says something, or you hear a song, or you even *smell* something, and you feel yourself immediately reminded of your loved one and suddenly feel like you want to cry. Sometimes you'll just start crying for no apparent reason.

This has happened to me several times since my dad died. In my case, it usually isn't until later that I realize the reason I'm crying, because the thing that triggers my grief attack seems completely unrelated at the time. This is definitely where the "weird" comes in for me. Things that other people might consider small or insignificant, things they may not even think twice about, sometimes make me feel overwhelmed with grief.

The first time this happened to me was one day when my mom and I were driving home from the hospital after we visited Dad. Although he was still alive, we knew he was getting worse — not better — and that he was probably dying. We had been talking about how he was doing, and I felt fine, emotionally. My eyes were not watery, and I felt in control of my feelings. I thought for sure I wasn't going to cry before we got home, until I mentioned something to my mom that I heard at school that day. Apparently, the owner of King Richard's (the local amusement park I had often gone to when I was younger) was thinking of selling his property and closing the business.

When I had heard the news earlier that day, I had hoped the park wouldn't close, but I wasn't terribly upset. When my mom and I were in the car, I suddenly remembered this and felt the need to tell her. As I started to open my mouth, I felt my eyes water and my throat clench. I tried to make my voice sound normal. "By the way," I said, "King Richard's is closing." I immediately started crying, but I didn't know why. I was fine with the thought earlier at school!

Then I realized that I was sad because my dad had taken me there so many times. He took me on my very first roller-coaster ride at King Richard's. He taught me how to drive a miniature racecar around their track. Many times he drove me to friends' birthday parties at King Richard's, and he would join the party and have as much fun as the kids, cruising around the racetrack and devouring slices of birthday cake. I now recognize this as my first grief attack. (By the way, the owner of King Richard's changed his mind and decided to keep the park open, and of that I am very glad.)

Another grief attack happened just weeks after Dad died. I was getting all dressed up for my friend Geena's bat mitzvah (a huge Jewish celebration of her thirteenth birthday). As I put on a new pair of sandals, I realized I should polish my toenails. Suddenly, I felt very sad and began to cry uncontrollably. I didn't want to take off the remnants of old nail polish because those flecks of blue had been there since before my dad died. As long as I had the old nail polish on, Dad seemed like he had just been in my life recently. I worried that taking it off would remove me from this safe part of my life where Dad had been alive.

I'm not sure how much time went by, but eventually I came up with a plan: I'd paint over the old polish using a light pink color. That way, I'd still be able to see the splotches of blue underneath. I stopped crying because I realized that I wouldn't be taking the nail polish *off*. I'd still have a piece of the old nail polish with me — another emotional connection to my dad — until it came off on its own. Something as simple as nail polish was enough to cause my grief attack.

It is important to know that you don't need to feel embarrassed when you have a grief attack. You might be perfectly happy until you walk into a room and see, say, smell, or hear something that unexpectedly upsets you. You are not the only one who goes through things like this. I know from experience that sometimes it seems easier to hide your tears when you suddenly feel sad in public, which is okay once in a while. But, if you do choose to hide your grief at times, it is important that you do share it with somebody later on, or maybe express it by writing in a journal.

Another example, one day soon after my dad's death, is when some friends and I were watching a DVD that my dad had loved. It was a rather unconventional musical animation film that he proudly showed *his* friends when they visited. I was happy that I was carrying on his tradition by introducing this unique movie to *my* friends. Then one person began to jokingly insult the movie. I knew that person didn't intend to be mean, but suddenly I thought about how much my dad had always loved that movie and then I felt my eyes well up. I spent most of the movie biting my lip so I wouldn't cry, because I didn't want everyone to see me crying about something like that.

Later that day, I thought about how oblivious to my feelings my friend had been and how his mocking Dad's favorite film had made me feel so sad. Now, looking back, even if I had let myself cry openly, I'm sure that my friends would have understood and comforted me, especially since it had only been a few months since my dad had died. You never need to feel embarrassed about what you are feeling. If you tell someone you trust how you feel, they will understand.

I've read self-help books that say people of any age can become emotionally scarred if they keep all their emotions pent up. Like the above example, it is sometimes okay to save your tears for later, as long as you eventually give them a chance to come out. When you hold back your emotions, it is like you are holding your breath. If you are in a situation where you think it's best not to breathe, you can hold your breath, but you need to let out that breath before you can breathe again. You can't inhale a fresh breath until you let out the old one, just like you can't bring in happy emotions until you make room for them by getting rid of the sad ones.

Sometimes I can't hold back the tears, no matter how hard I try. Each fall my school hosts its annual harvest-themed event that my dad helped out with in past years. Dad usually volunteered to take little kids on pony rides or run one of the carnival games, like miniature boat races. The first year I went to the event after Dad died, I was a little teary at first. But once we got there I began to warm up to the event. After I wandered around the school for a bit, however, I started to cry. They had switched the management of the event, and several of the traditional stalls and activities were missing.

Two of my favorite teachers were standing with my mom, and they asked me why I looked so sad. I told them that this year's Harvest Hay Day was really different from the years when Dad was there. My teachers validated that it must be hard going to that event for the first time since my dad died. Their understanding helped, and I went home feeling better about it.

When you are talking to people about your loved one, it is okay if you cry. I can't emphasize enough that tears don't make you a baby, or weak, or anything else negative; they only let out the pain and grief you are feeling. If you are talking to someone you trust, you definitely don't have to hide your tears. It is better in the long run if you let out your tears with someone, because some people who bottle up their feelings can be prone to high stress or bursts of anger later on. For teenagers, life can sometimes be stressful enough as it is!

At a GLance:

• *Nothing is wrong with you if your grieving patterns are different from those of adults — for teenagers they can be unpredictable, and this often seems weird.*

• *Grief attacks occur when unexpected waves of grief come crashing down upon us.*

• *When a grief attack hits, you might feel trapped in a situation, afraid to show your emotions. Hiding your tears is okay in some circumstances as long as you remember to share your grief later with a person you trust.*

• *You don't have to feel embarrassed about grief attacks; everyone who has experienced a painful loss has had them.*

• *Tears help let the pain out; they aren't a meter showing how emotionally strong we are.*

• *Before you can let in happy feelings, you must first let out the emotions that come with grief, just like you can't inhale a fresh breath until you exhale the old one.*

• *Bottling up our feelings isn't healthy and can lead to bursts of anger later.*

Chapter 6

From TeenaGers to Adults

You might think it's strange when you don't always cry when adults do, yet you suddenly feel overwhelmed with emotion over something relatively small. I have dealt with the same thing. Adults often become emotional over something that reminds them of the loved one they miss, whether it's the mention of his or her name or just looking at something the loved one gave to them. I know that one of the most emotional reminders for my mom is when she hears music that she and my dad would listen to or dance to.

You might also think that examples like that are "the normal thing" because that's the way some adults grieve, and no one talks about it being any different. The truth is that, as I have experienced, for teenagers it can be very different. Between my mom and me, we cover a lot of ground when it comes to different grief attacks. I find that for me, and probably a lot of teenagers, the little things get me more than the obvious ones, which is different from how my mom deals with things concerning grief. The following example is probably the weirdest that comes to mind.

At the time, I wasn't even thinking of my dad; I was getting ready to heat up leftovers in one of our microwave ovens. I was about to put my plate of cold food into the little spare microwave that sits in the corner of our counter (my mom was using the bigger one) when I noticed its digital clock wasn't working. I mentioned this to my mom, who said that it might have burned itself out. I instantly felt a strong attachment to that microwave; I hoped it hadn't stopped working. I went into the garage and reset the circuit breaker, thinking that we might have had a power outage. I came back inside to see that the microwave still wasn't displaying its little glowing numbers.

I tried to reason how long microwave ovens lasted and how long we had had this one. I started crying when my mom said that this one might have died and we should probably put it out for tomorrow's trash day. I explained that I didn't know why I was crying, and then I looked over at the microwave to see its little digital screen light up. "Mom," I called, "the microwave's working!" Knowing that we could keep our little microwave oven, I continued to cry although now I was relieved and happy.

I didn't really know why I was crying until I thought about Dad, realizing that he used the little microwave most of the time. I could picture him humming as he placed his TV dinner of turkey and gravy or macaroni and cheese into the microwave oven, stopping to pet one of our cats or to tell me an interesting fact about science or nature. I then realized I was crying because I missed my dad, and this hunk of metal, wires, and high-tech gadgetry represented a strong connection to him.

If you and an adult friend or family member are both grieving, compare the differences between your grief attacks. This will help you both learn to tune into each other's feelings and know when to comfort each other. Talk about how your grief differs from that of other people. I sometimes get sad when I think I can't keep something that reminds me of Dad — weird things like King Richard's amusement park, my nail polish, or the little microwave oven — while my mom's memories of him are triggered by so-called "normal" things like hearing songs they used to dance to.

At a GLance:

• *Adults tend to have more obvious grief attack triggers than teenagers do.*

• *Sometimes grief attacks seem silly or spontaneous; you might not know you're grieving your loved one until later.*

- *Your grief attacks don't have to be similar to those of adults; try talking to a family member or other person who is also grieving about these differences. This will help you both learn to tune into each other's feelings and comfort each other.*

PART III: On the HealinG Road to PEace

IntRoduction

An important goal for me on my grief journey has been getting to the point where I feel at peace and happy again. Even though I will forever remember my loved ones who died, and it won't be the same without them — especially my dad — I think it's important to give myself the opportunity to heal inside and be able to come to terms with my grief. This will allow me to find my norm again and get back to everyday life.

I think we can achieve this goal gradually by talking about our loss and our feelings with someone close or by expressing ourselves creatively. We can also make remembering our loved ones part of our everyday life, instead of just waiting for anniversaries or holidays.

Chapter 7

Talk ABout It

I really can't stress enough how important talking about my grief has been for me. It has helped me the most. I suggest it to you, whether you are accustomed to sharing your feelings or not. I suggest talking to at least one person — a mom or dad, cousin, best friend, brother or sister, neighbor, teacher, school counselor, or anyone else you trust — about how you *really* feel. Even if it's hard for you to talk about the way you feel, it's important in healing your grief that you try to talk to someone.

When I talk to somebody about what makes me sad or happy or what reminds me of my dad, I feel like I have support and somebody who better understands what I'm going through. For me, this special person is my mom. If there is something that I feel strongly about on a particular day, I make a mental note to tell my mom about it later.

You may be thinking, "Nobody knows how I feel!" Keep in mind that almost everybody has grieved at some point in life. Though the person might not know exactly how you feel, if you take the time to explain your feelings about your loved one to someone, he or she will be closer to understanding what you feel. Having someone understand where you're coming from makes you feel better.

What I think people often forget is that teenagers grieve differently and often have a wider range of feelings a lot of the time, *especially* when we're grieving. When we can talk about our emotions and know that it's okay to feel all of those crazy feelings, then we can truly heal. Plus, not only will you feel your heart begin to heal, but you will also become closer to the person with whom you decide to share this.

Try to find someone to talk to who knew your loved one. I like to talk with my mom about the feelings I have about Dad. We both knew him so well. We both have insights about things we could do to remember him in ways that would make him proud of us. We also tell each other how we grieve, and we talk about what different things make us remember Dad or bring us face-to-face with our grief.

You aren't helping anyone, especially yourself, if you hide your grief and feelings inside. You only rob yourself of the opportunities to share your emotions, and sharing your emotions helps you to heal. I know it's hard to believe, but in time, you can heal from all kinds of grief and go back to living peacefully, even if you still think often about the person you lost and miss them.

Always remember that you can talk with *someone* about your grief. Once they understand where you're coming from, they will respect your feelings. Again, grief isn't something to be embarrassed about.

It might seem like simply talking about how you feel wouldn't help your grief, but trust me; just being heard can make all the difference in the world. From experiences some of my friends have had, I also know that it takes much longer to heal your heart and get back to everyday life if you *aren't* willing to share your feelings. If I am feeling sad about my dad or just extra-emotional because something reminds me of him, I definitely feel better when I just get it out there and talk about it.

That special person you feel comfortable talking to will understand if you let your feelings out. Most people don't mind if you talk about your loved one with them. Sorting out your feelings and getting another opinion about how you can feel better will help heal your grief, and it will eventually help you to come to terms with your loss and feel better about expressing your feelings about that person. My mom and I are proof of this!

It's especially helpful to talk with someone else who is grieving, because sharing your experiences with others in your situation helps you realize that you're not alone. Whether this is a friend, parent, or somebody else, it really helps to talk to someone to share insights and stories about your grief process. You might also find it easier to talk to a family member about grief because they might be grieving about the same person or pet that you are.

Or, you might consider asking your friends how they have grieved. Some may say that they have lost a dog, a grandparent, or a friend. They might have even experienced the same loss you have (like two people losing their grandfathers), in which case you can help each other a lot just by relating to each other. You can talk about your experiences with grief attacks, how you like to remember that person, and simply how you feel!

I now know several teenagers around my age group at school who lost their dads, too. I know how good it feels to be able to talk with someone else who has lost a dad. In turn, I have offered my ear to someone else who lost his dad after I lost mine. Even if you may not think so, someone may have experienced a loss but chooses not to share it or show it. If a peer of yours is grieving, he or she might know more about what you are feeling than you think. You can always ask; you might be surprised to know how many people want to share their own stories to help you and give you advice.

Sharing with another grieving person whether you feel sad, upset, numb, or anything else — then listening to their side — is very healing. If the other person is more distressed than you are, you can feel fortunate to be where you are in your grief journey. In turn, you can help the person with whatever he or she is dealing with.

On the other hand, if there is something that you are not as good at handling, you can ask that person how he or she deals with that area of grieving so well. I think you will find that sharing stories and feelings about grief and your loved one who died will help you identify your feelings, allowing you to cope with your grief more easily and eventually heal.

I know that right after a loved one's death it might seem like things will *never* get back to normal and that you will *always* feel sad, but trust me when I say that you will adjust to the loss, and life will start to seem more normal again. It is true that things will never be the same, but you will be able to get back to your everyday life. You will eventually come to a place where you welcome thoughts and feelings of that person.

I can mention my dad more easily now because I have already let out so many feelings. Everyone is different, so don't pressure yourself to feel how other people might feel in your circumstances; you will be able to find your own "normal" state again in your own way and in your own time. Always remember that there is no timeline when it comes to grief!

At a GLance:

- *Talk about it; try to find at least one person who you can talk with openly to help you heal.*

- *Almost everybody has grieved at some point and will be able to relate to you on some level.*

- *Talking about our emotions helps us to know it's okay to feel all those crazy feelings!*

- *If you know someone else who is grieving, sharing with them helps you realize you're not alone. And you can help each other heal!*

- *Someday you will feel "back to normal," at peace, and happy again.*

- *Things will never be exactly the same after your loss, but that doesn't mean you won't be happy again.*

Chapter 8

RememBerinG Your LoVed One

I think that a part of grieving many people find difficult is remembering a loved one and including him or her in their daily lives, even though he or she is not around physically. This can sometimes be hard because thinking about your loved one can stir up feelings you had forgotten about. You might feel really sad at first, but thinking of your loved one like this is actually good in the long run. You will feel better, lighter, once you do something to remember your loved one.

One thing I have done and you might want to consider doing for your loved one who died is putting together pictures of him or her to share with your friends and family. This could be a personal thing for you to share with just a few people, or it could be in relation to a funeral or memorial service. Holding a celebration of his or her life, rather than a regular funeral, can really help people to feel better about their grief. You don't have to put on a big event with a lot of guests. Just putting together some pictures of your loved one, books, or other things that he or she had liked is enough of a memorial to honor him or her.

Another activity that I found really helps me to get through hard times, like the "first holidays," is to get together with one or two (or more) people and actually do something that my dad liked to do. For the first Father's Day after my dad died, my mom and I got up early to watch the Formula One car race, which Dad loved doing. Then we drove *his* car to Home Depot, one of his favorite stores because he enjoyed doing handyman projects around the house. This made Father's Day much easier for both my mom and me because we were remembering him in a fun way. I find that doing something fun that has to do with your beloved person or pet takes your mind off of sad feelings and helps you heal.

I continue to do things such as this on days like Father's Day or my dad's birthday. We celebrate him in ways that are fun for us, too. Even when it isn't a first holiday, it's still meaningful to get together and do activities that your loved one enjoyed. You can heal your grief as you remember happy times together.

I also find that it makes me feel better when I can walk around the house and see things that had belonged to my dad, rather than shutting all his stuff away. Having things around the house that remind you of your loved one helps you not to become overwhelmed with grief if you accidentally come across something that reminds you of that person. It helps you get used to being reminded of this person, so you can feel okay when things like that are seen unexpectedly. Also, you don't have to forget about your loved one completely by shutting all the memories away — he or she can remain a part of your life. For example, I have a picture of my dad on the shelf above our fireplace. Every time I walk into the room, I see my dad's face. If other family members don't want pictures to stay up, you could keep pictures or special items in your room.

For me, an important step in healing after a loss is being able to talk happily about the person who died, but I had to grieve a fair amount before I could do this comfortably. This sometimes means crying and letting out the feelings that need to get out. It is okay if you feel sad when you do things that remind you of your loved one. You are allowed to feel sad.

However, if you feel you are not ready to talk about remembering your loved one, that's okay, too. If you aren't ready, make sure to share or let out your feelings in other ways you *are* ready for, so someday you will be able to freely talk about your special person and feel at peace and happy. This doesn't happen all at once. The best way to do this is to let out your feelings in intervals you feel comfortable with.

As I see it, letting out your feelings is sort of like going to a carnival. You want to go on some rides, or else when you get home you will feel disappointed that you didn't get to release any of the excitement that built up when you were there. You also don't want to go on rides that are too scary for you, because that won't be fun if you aren't ready for them yet.

What you want to do is go on the rides you feel comfortable with, while stretching your comfort zone a little bit at a time. Grieving is similar. If you don't grieve at all, then your feelings will be built up inside of you, and you might cry at just the mention of the person's name and won't want to talk about him or her at all.

On the other hand, you don't want to participate in activities that scratch surfaces that are too raw by making you relive things too soon. The best route is in the middle, where you might start by talking about how great the person or pet was, working up to doing things to remember them or laughing at jokes and memories. It is okay if you cry at first, or even later on, but I think you will find that as you gradually vent your feelings, you will feel more comfortable mentioning this person and including his or her memory in your everyday life.

At a GLance:

- *Including reminders of your loved one in your daily life will help you adjust to the loss but still keep that person in your life.*

- *Doing something your loved one loved to do helps make "first holidays" less painful.*

- *Remembering happy times spent with your loved one is another way to heal and begin to feel comfortable talking about that person or pet again.*

- *If you are not ready to engage in a specific activity that reminds you of your loved one, then try something that feels more comfortable, stretching your comfort zone when you are ready.*

PART IV: SiGɔs of Continued LoVe

IntRoduction

I truly believe that my dad, grandma, grandpas, and your loved ones are never really gone, that their souls live on forever. I also believe that after a loved one dies, they send us signs of their continued love to let us know they are with us in spirit. Some people might believe that these signs of continued love are not really signs, just meaningless coincidences, and that our loved ones are really gone. I don't feel that this is true at all!

I hope you stay open to what I'm saying in this next section. It's okay if you think this is crazy at first. Even if you don't feel your loved one's presence right now, hang in with me, and at least read the next chapter to see if any of the examples I share ring true for you. Please don't feel like I am asking you to drastically change your beliefs. I'm just sharing with you the experiences I've had that have helped me stay connected to the love of those who have died, especially my dad.

Chapter 9

Look AnywheRe for SiGns of Continued LoVe

igns of continued love are messages from your loved one who has died, telling you he or she is still around in spirit and will be with you always. These come in any way, shape, or form, so keep your eyes, ears, mind, and heart open to these incidences, which can also be called coincidences or synchronicities. Signs don't have to be huge or obvious to everyone; they just have to be special to you!

Do not let anyone convince you that your loved one is simply gone. I believe they are with you everywhere you go. If you feel the presence of your loved one or see something repeatedly, like a favorite animal or something of special meaning to your loved one — or even something that is special to you — *pay attention to it.* Don't just think, "I must be imagining it because I am thinking about my loved one so much," or, "I must be going crazy."

Signs from loved ones aren't always big, huge, supernatural, or out of the ordinary, although they can be any of those things. Some people say they haven't received any signs yet simply because they might have been looking for loud, bright fireworks in the sky rather than a small heart-shaped leaf on the ground, a meaningful pattern in the sand, or a familiar shape in a cloud. Sure, you could get fireworks in the sky spelling your loved one's name, but you aren't going to see that if you don't learn to notice the small things first.

Signs of continued love come large and small, from completely, hilariously obvious to cheerfully discreet. One benefit that we have as teenagers is that we are often willing to look closer than adults do. While adults might go around blind, walking right into signs they don't even see, we can look anywhere — in a store, on the desk, on the floor, at the beach — and we see signs! I will describe a few of my own, some big and some small, to give you an idea of how someone comes to see signs frequently.

I started seeing signs when I was 5 years old after my grandpas both died within just a few weeks. The signs from Grampa Dutch and Grandpa Wheeler were always heart-shaped. I'd see heart-shaped stones, puddles, leaves, bubbles — you name it — and each time I knew these were from my grandpas, telling me they still loved me. I even saw heart-shaped bread-and-butter pickle slices, which is why my mom wrote a children's grief support book, called *Heart-Shaped Pickles*.

For years I saw hearts everywhere, and even today I'll notice a heart shape in some unexpected way and think about my grandfathers. Then, when I was 11 and my grandmother died, I started seeing yellow butterflies whenever I thought about her and how much I missed being with her. I think she sent me yellow butterflies as a reminder of her love because they were her favorite type of butterfly, and she often pointed them out to me when we played together outside.

Now I can't wait to tell you about the two most frequent signs I receive from my dad, which are frogs and dragonflies. The weird (but cool!) thing is that my mom and I see frogs and dragonflies *everywhere,* even in places where someone wouldn't expect to come across anything of the sort!

The last outing (other than the hospital) that my dad had, even though he didn't know it at the time, was when my mom, dad, a couple of friends, and I were going out to dinner at a restaurant downtown. My dad wasn't feeling well — he had a stomachache — but he insisted that he drive us home, even in the pouring rain. It was dark out by the time we reached our neighborhood, and as we pulled up into our long driveway, my dad suddenly slammed on the brakes, and we all lurched forward. He said, "Whoa! Did you two see that *huge* frog?" Soon the frog was hopping in front of our car and safely across puddles in the driveway. Ever since then, at significant moments relating to my dad, I find frogs in unexpected places. I see them on our patio, hopping into gardens at the park, or pictures of frogs on billboards and in my school textbooks. I'll be thinking about Dad or telling my friend one of his many favorite jokes, and when I look up (or down), there's a frog!

The dragonflies came to be symbolic for me soon after my dad knew he was sick. He went to the mall one day and came home humming the "Happy Birthday" song to my mom. He hid a bag in his closet, where he always hid presents. It was a bit odd at the time, because my mom's birthday wasn't for a couple months. Plus, my dad had always been a last-minute shopper (you probably know someone like this), stopping to get gifts, a greeting card, or flowers the day of a birthday or anniversary.

The very next day, my dad announced to my mom that he wanted to give her an early birthday present. He had been giving my mom heart-shaped silver jewelry from their favorite jewelry store for anniversaries and birthdays, but this time he gave my mom a beautiful dragonfly pin. He explained that it just jumped out at him, so he bought it, and he had a strong feeling he needed to give it to her right then. The pin had eight tiny diamonds on its body, my mom's lucky number.

It turned out that my dad never lived to see my mom's actual birthday. He went into the hospital a few days after he gave her the pin, and he never came back home again. My mom wears the pin almost every day, whether she is going shopping or dressing up for a business conference. And ever since she got it, I see dragonflies *everywhere!* I even saw them when my dad was still in the hospital.

One day after visiting Dad in the Intensive Care Unit, I could tell his illness was much worse and that he was probably dying. As my mom and I got into the elevator, she asked me what I was thinking and feeling. I told her it was like part of Dad was already in Heaven. She said she felt the same thing. We were both sobbing as we walked down the long hallway toward the exit to the parking lot. The sliding doors opened, we stepped out into the parking lot and, through our blur of tears, we saw thousands of dragonflies. It was like a parade of them in the sky! Then I noticed they were only flying right around us. I could see no other dragonflies dancing in other parts of the big parking lot.

Every time I see a frog or dragonfly I know it is a sign from my dad, especially if it is in an unlikely place, like a huge frog I found in our watering can and a dragonfly I saw land on a turtle's nose sticking out of the water. A dragonfly on a turtle's nose! Really, Dad.

Now here's a huge, hilariously obvious kind of story, the kind that Mom and her friends call "woo-woos." Woo-woos are signs that you can tell anybody about, and they will recognize that something is going on here that is much more than a simple coincidence. This sign happened one day in early December when my mom and I traveled to California to speak about grief. The whole reason we were there was to share our experiences after Dad's death, read from some of my mom's grief support books, and tell people about signs of continued love (or "comforting coincidences," as my mom likes to call them) that come to us, both large and small.

My mom and I got into our hotel the night before we were supposed to speak. We went upstairs, set down our luggage, and conked off to sleep. In the morning, we went downstairs to eat breakfast. As we sat down at our table in the lobby to eat, I admired the huge Christmas tree and all of the hotel's other holiday decorations.

Suddenly, we heard this loud, scratchy noise — an animal call. At first, something in my head said, "I know it's a frog." My lips started to curl into a smile, but I kept listening just to be sure. It sounded like it could be either a large bird or a frog. It wasn't exactly like a "ribbit," but more like a long, loud, scratchy croak.

I turned to my mom and asked, "Is that a frog?" My mom just smiled, and we both looked around the lobby to see where the sound was coming from. It seemed to come from either the ceiling or the top of the Christmas tree. Other guests were looking up at the chandelier, then to the Christmas tree, trying to figure out what was making this odd sound. One of the guests said, "Okay, I give up. What is it?" Mom and I laughed.

Mom then walked up to the desk to ask about it, and I was hoping it was a frog! The lady at the front desk immediately apologized. "I'm so sorry. That's our tree frog. We can't find him to get him out of the lobby, and he does this every so often. I'm so sorry he disturbed your breakfast! People complain all the time!"

When Mom came and told me that it was a tree frog, we both laughed so hysterically that we didn't know what to say. We might as well have seen a huge billboard with the headline, "Dad loves you!" I imagine the small print on the billboard would say, "And he is so proud of you and Mom for traveling to speak with other grieving people."

The frog didn't make its call again that morning or the whole rest of our visit. It only croaked the morning we were supposed to speak with people about grief, which was the first time we had publicly shared our experiences since Dad died! I had a whole new story about signs of continued love to tell to our grief group, and it also helped me get through the holiday season.

Now, another crazy thing is that I see certain patterns of numbers on clocks. Dad was good at computer programming and loved working with numbers. Ever since he died, I'll look up at a clock and notice that it's 7:11 (my birthday, July 11), 3:55 (the time of day at which my dad died), 9:11 (the day my dad went to the hospital, September 11), or double, triple, even quadruple digits such as 3:33, 1:11, and 11:11. These are signs that I catch often, and I feel the presence of my dad with me especially when I see these.

Even right now as I am typing this paragraph on my computer, I am looking up at Dad's 24-hour clock in his old office that shows military time (like 13:00 rather than 1:00 p.m.), and I see 17:11! Not only does that have my birth date in it, but an extra number one! That's 7:11, plus triple ones!

Some people like to explain away these signs, but really, how many times each day does one person look up and see these number combinations? I know that the special part about seeing these double and triple digits is that Dad is inspiring me to continue to work on my book and to look up right when these special patterns appear.

Signs don't always have to shout your name in flying colors; they simply have to make you think of your loved one, and you have to know that they are from that person or pet. Recently, I was sitting home alone writing this book while my mom was at work. It had been a year and a half since my dad died, and we had pretty much stopped getting calls and e-mails for him, although we still got some junkmail in the mailbox addressed to him. The phone was ringing, and I don't have caller ID in the computer room, so I answered it.

A woman's voice said, "Hello, is Gary Wheeler there?" I almost laughed. My dad's name isn't Gary; it's Gerry. Most people misspell his name because they think it is spelled "Jerry." This lady obviously had the spelling correct but got the pronunciation all wrong. At that point I knew that it must be a sales call, so I just said, "I'm sorry, but he isn't at home right now. Goodbye," and hung up the phone. Like with the numbers on the clock, I knew that my dad was playing tricks on me.

Signs can also come to you at significant times to show you that what you are doing is good and that your loved one is helping you. Maybe your grandmother had a favorite flower, and just when you're feeling nervous about something like taking a test, you look over and see blossoms of that very same flower. Grandma is probably telling you she is right there with you!

Just today, while I was writing a section of this book on my computer in my dad's old office, a Dilbert figure suddenly fell off the shelf and landed on the desk in front of me. Dilbert was my dad's favorite cartoon character, and he kept three or four of them in his office. Nothing else fell off the shelf, and there wasn't any shaking, except probably Dad with laughter.

On the same day, as I wrote a section of this book and wondered if I should keep writing, the battery backups for my computer and my dad's old computer both started beeping. The power was flickering on and off, and I could hear the switch inside it click on and off, but my computer was unaffected. I knew this was my dad saying, "Keep writing!"

He always loved computers, and now I am using his "gadget room" (what my dad always called his computer room) to write this book on my computer, which is right next to his. I got the message to keep writing, and I didn't hear the battery backup beep again for the rest of the day.

When I walked into the computer room today, I saw a beautiful, curving rainbow circling around the ceiling of my dad's office. It was reflecting off of a CD-R stack on top of Dad's old computer. It wasn't the first rainbow I have seen. Rainbows appeared on significant days for my dad, like the day he went to the hospital, his birthday, and other times I was thinking of him. I often see "CD rainbows" in his office and know that they are from Dad because he was so high-tech. As I write this paragraph about CD rainbows, I see 3:55 on the clock again. I know that my dad is right here, helping me to write this book! Thanks, Dad. I love you.

At a GLance:

• *Signs come in many different ways as our loved ones try to tell us their love is still with us.*

• *Try to keep your eyes, ears, mind, and heart open to these special synchronicities.*

• *Signs don't have to be huge or obvious to* everyone; *they just have to be special to you.*

• *People sometimes try to explain away signs of continued love. When you see signs, it's not just your imagination; you aren't crazy!*

• *Pay attention if you see a favorite animal or something else of special meaning to your loved one.*

• *If you notice a sign while you are doing a particular activity, it can mean that your loved one approves of this (such as seeing Grandma's favorite flower while you are about to do something you are nervous about).*

Chapter 10

OpeninG YouRself to SiGns

I believe that teenagers naturally connect more easily to signs from Heaven, the "other side," or whatever you wish to call it, and to loved ones who have died because, like with children, we have not yet been taught how to think according to social norms. For most of us, society hasn't yet molded us into thinking that our loved one is simply "in a better place now," and that is that. We are more open to the fact that he or she, even though no longer in physical form, is always with us in spirit form and can still communicate with loved ones on Earth if they stay open.

In fact, I think teenagers and children have a special gift in this area. We are more accepting of out-of-the ordinary experiences than grownups, because adults tend to explain them away, thinking, "I must be imagining this." It's almost automatic, I think, for many adults to rationalize things and explain away odd incidences.

If you see signs, don't let anyone tell you that your loved one is just "gone," because he or she isn't! If we stay open to receiving signs of continued love from our loved ones as teenagers, I think we will be more likely to stay open to these things as adults. Sure, adults can open up to these signs, too, but it's easier if you have already experienced this openness at a young age.

As I mentioned before, these signs don't have to be sure signs to everybody — just you — so don't get discouraged if the person standing next to you thinks that the sign isn't from your loved one. Our loved ones send us signs that they know we will recognize, so if you notice a sign that reminds you of your loved one, know it is from them. Don't let anyone tell you that you are just thinking about this person too much, or that you're crazy, because you're not. You just need to be *open* to receiving signs in order to start *seeing* them.

Signs from loved ones come differently to everyone. If you don't know where to start, try paying attention enough to notice if you see or hear things more often since your loved one died, like his or her favorite animal, object, song, or flower, for example. If you do, chances are these things have to do with that person. If the loved one you lost was a pet, in which case you might not know exactly what their favorite things were, signs might come to you in the form of toys or pictures of that animal that show up unexpectedly, or seeing things like hearts or other significant objects when someone is talking about your pet.

If every time you walk into a room or new place you think, even in the back of your mind, "I *know* I will see a sign from my loved one soon," then you will start seeing them by staying open. If you always have the thought of a sign tucked in the back of your mind, then you will be more likely to receive signs because you are willing to look carefully. You don't have to go looking for signs; you just have to be open to their possibility and know that your loved one will send you the signs you need.

Another way to keep yourself open to signs is to ask your loved one to help you with things. For example, if you want to see a sign, tell your loved one in your mind, "I want to see a sign from you today. Please let me see one." If you say this and *mean* it — and know that your loved one will listen to you, whether he or she will get back to you with the answer right away or not — then you will begin to see how your loved one is still helping you, maybe even more than when he or she was in your life physically. Don't be disappointed if you don't see the sign right away, because your loved one is working on it and has to find a way to fit the sign into your life so that you can notice it.

The more signs you see, like my frogs, rainbows, and dragonflies, the easier this becomes, because you get better at noticing the signs your loved one sends to you. If you just keep expecting a sign that you will know is from your loved one, it will become easier for your loved one to show you signs because you will notice them. Part of receiving signs is having your loved one "tell you" to look up at just the right time so you see something from them. If you listen to your intuition and follow the feelings that you are meant to do something, then you will notice more signs from your loved ones. For instance, if you feel as if someone was tapping on your shoulder, as if someone wanted you to look in a certain direction, or if you just feel an unexplainable urge to go in a particular grocery aisle or something like that, try following it. I bet you will be more likely to see meaningful items and symbols.

One day while I was shopping for materials for a school project at the craft store, I noticed an aisle of wind chimes. I got a feeling of knowing, and at that moment I was sure there would be frogs and dragonflies in that aisle. I looked into the aisle and saw that more than half of the wind chimes in that aisle and the next one had frogs, dragonflies, or both! I couldn't believe my eyes. I bought two or three wind chimes, and I still have them. Whenever I hear them chime I picture my dad laughing or smiling at me.

Follow your intuition, and listen carefully with your heart as well as with your head for directions from your loved one. These don't have to sound like actual words, necessarily, but if you feel a sort of pulling toward a certain place, almost like someone is pointing for you to look, then *look!* This is most likely your loved one telling you that you are meant to see something.

I hope that you find signs from your loved one who died, just as I see frogs and dragonflies from my dad. Stay open to noticing these signs and I promise you that in time you will see even more! And the signs will probably make you smile — maybe even laugh!

At a GLance:

- *Although your loved one may not be around physically, he or she can still communicate with you if you stay open to signs they send you.*

- *As teens, we have the special gift of naturally accepting out-of-the ordinary experiences like seeing signs of continued love.*

- *If you stay open now, you will most likely be able to see signs frequently as an adult.*

- *When you walk into a room or a new place, try telling yourself, "I know I will see a sign…"*

- *You can even ask your loved one to help you recognize signs.*

- *The more your heart opens to the possibility of signs, the more signs you are likely to see.*

- *Be prepared to see signs that you didn't expect.*

- *Let your intuition be your guide.*

- *Don't be afraid to laugh!*

Thanks, Dad, for helping me stay open to laughter along my grief journey. Keep those weird and wacky signs coming!

And to you, I want to say, *congratulations!* You did it! You have taken a step (whether or not it is the first one) toward healing your grief, simply by reading this book. I hope that you will feel okay with "where you are at" in your grief journey and understand that no matter how you grieve or how long it takes for life to seem normal again, try to keep expressing yourself in one way or another. You will get through this journey somehow, even if it is weird at times. I hope you know that there are *many* teens going through similar things, and I hope this book has helped you by allowing you to see at least one teen's experiences. Good luck! And feel free to email me if you want to share your own stories and experiences. Just email Jenny@WeirdisNormal.org. I can't promise I will be able to answer every email, but please know that I will try my best.

AfterwoRd: How LauGhter Helped OuR Family

hello, readers. This is Jenny's mom. Because Jenny shared so openly with you about how her dad sends her signs of continued love that make her laugh, I wanted to tell you more about how laughter helped our family during our time of tragedy and loss.

In our society it seems like death is such a heavy, sad subject, and I think that many people — especially adults — think our grief journey needs to be that way, too.

Jenny has helped me realize this doesn't have to be the case. I remember when Jenny first started seeing hearts in unexpected ways after her grandpas died, and how each sighting made her smile, even laugh. She would tell us she believed these were signs from her grandpas: "Now I know they're together, and they still love all of us." Her dad and I were really sad back then. Losing both of our fathers within a few weeks of each other was extremely hard for us. But whenever Jenny pointed out a heart-shaped cloud or heart-shaped puddle to us, it made us smile, too!

The signs Jenny's dad sends her — especially frogs — often are funny or even hilarious to her. He had a wacky sense of humor, so maybe that's why he chooses to send signs that are lighthearted. I guess maybe he wants to help lighten her heart as she grieves.

I'm going to tell you the story of how her dad was finally able to take his last breath and make his "transition" in peace, because humor played a big part on that October afternoon. *Transition* is the word we use in our family when someone dies because we believe when their body dies, their soul lives on, so at death they transition back into pure spirit form.

As Jenny mentioned in Chapter 1, one day her dad was perfectly healthy, and within a month, he was dying of advanced cancer. We knew his Earth walk was coming to a completion. As we gathered around his hospital bed, the nurses said he might live for just a few minutes once they removed the breathing machine, because his disease was keeping his lungs from working on their own. Even though he was unconscious, the nurses reminded us that hearing is the last sense to go, so we shouldn't hesitate to talk to him.

I held his right hand, and Jenny held his left as we huddled as close as we could get to this man we loved so dearly. Other family members gathered right there with us. Tears flowed silently as we stifled our natural inclination to break out in uncontrollable sobs of grief.

Because I have been a hospice volunteer, visiting with patients who were dying, I took the lead, talking out loud to my husband Gerry. I kept telling him how much we all loved him; how we all thanked him for being such a wonderful husband, father, son, brother, brother-in-law; and how we would never forget him. I gave him permission to go, saying things like, "Whenever it's your time, it's okay to go, Gerry. Go in peace. Go with our love." Often, Jenny chimed in, too, telling him over and over again, "I love you, Dad. Thank you, Dad. I'll miss you, Dad."

Well, I guess Gerry wasn't ready to go, because he hung on by a thread for almost an hour. Just when we all thought he had taken his last breath and his heart had stopped beating, a minute or so would go by, and he'd suddenly start breathing once again. This happened several times, and the anguish for all of us was so intense that I started crying so hard I couldn't whisper another word to him.

The heavy anticipation in that room was so overwhelming that none of us knew what to do. Next thing I knew, Jenny was reaching over to pick up the little stuffed toy frog she had given her dad after he was moved from a regular hospital bed to the Intensive Care Unit. It's one of those toys with a sound button. Jenny pushed the button on the frog's belly, and the room echoed with "Ribbit, ribbit, ribbit, ribbit."

We all burst out into laughter. The doom and gloom in the tiny ICU room seemed to lift. I started talking to Gerry about signs of continued love. "Be sure to send us lots of signs," I told him.

Just two weeks earlier, when it was clear his life was coming to an end, I asked Gerry what kind of signs he thought he might send. He scratched his beard for a few seconds — his way of showing me he was deep in thought — and replied, "Well, I don't know. It's not like you're given a manual and can turn to the chapter on signs to see what all the choices will be." Typical Gerry, giving me a scientific answer!

My sister Jan, who had a very special bond with Gerry — they loved to discuss science fiction and all kinds of subjects — was sitting behind Jenny in the ICU so she could be close to Jenny to give her hugs and support. At my mention of signs, Jan piped up, kidding Gerry that she couldn't wait to see what kinds of clever signs he'd come up with to send to all of us. Again, amidst our tears, we all grinned.

"But keep the signs simple so I get them," I added. "Things like hearts, frogs, and dragonflies are okay, but don't send me anything too tricky or complicated. You know how I never even get the punch lines of your jokes."

Then Jenny leaned over, and in between smiles and tears, she told him, "But it's okay, Dad. You can send *me* the tricky ones. I'll be able to figure them out." For the next few minutes, the words we shared with Gerry now included *laughter.* We told him how much we loved him. And we thanked him for his love, his life, *and* his laughter. Especially all the years of laughter!

The room seemed to glow brightly. Without any more struggle to try to stay alive, Gerry finally took his last breath and died peacefully. He made his transition in a room that was overflowing with love *and* laughter.

I believe Gerry somehow inspired Jenny to pick up that little frog, press its belly, and help shift the energy in the hospital room from heavy sorrow to smiles and gratitude. After all, Gerry didn't live his life in sad, somber ways — just the opposite! So he certainly wouldn't have wanted to make his transition surrounded by people who were overwhelmed by sadness.

Thank you for letting me tell you this story. For me, it shows that laughter has a place in our lives, even when facing death. And it also underscores how kids and teens — just by being themselves and following their perfect inner guidance systems — can bring hope when the world seems to be filled with nothing but despair.

— *Karla Wheeler, Naples, Florida*

HelpfuL WeBsites

Jenny has found many websites with helpful information for grieving teens. Because website addresses change or become outdated, she has decided to list them on her website. Please visit **www.WeirdisNormal.org** and click on the link, "Helpful Websites." If you know of sites that she hasn't included, please email your suggestions to her: Jenny@WeirdisNormal.org. Thanks!

AcknowledGments

I would like to thank everyone who was so supportive while my dad was sick and after he died. Every little thing that someone did or said made a positive difference! So, thank you to everyone at Seacrest School (teachers, staff, and classmates), neighbors, friends, and family — either here in the U.S. or in Canada, my dad's home and native land.

Thanks, Mom, who encouraged me to write this book and has helped support me all along through this journey of inspiration, writing, and now publishing.

Thanks to everyone at Quality of Life Publishing, including Kelly Brachle, who designed the front and back covers and dedicated herself to the task of dragging and placing all the little words until they were perfect.

A big thank you to everyone who reviewed drafts of my manuscript and offered suggestions, especially Dr. Gloria Horsley and her daughter Dr. Heidi Horsley, who took the time to write the particularly insightful Foreword.

I most of all thank Dad for being the inspiration to write this book. Without him in my life I wouldn't know what it's like to have such a great dad, even though my dad was in my life for a shorter period of time than most. Thank you, Dad, for being witty, clever, supportive, fun, knowledgeable, and willing to share your intellect with me. Thanks also for your signs of continued love that you keep on sending my way, which have inspired me to write, and which encourage me every day. And, of course, thank you, Dad, for being in my life.

About the AuthoR

Jenny Lee Wheeler is no stranger to death. She was 5 when both her grandpas died, 11 when her grandma died, and 14 when her dad got sick and died a month later.

As Jenny began to grieve her dad's death, she noticed that she mourned differently from the adults around her. Jenny's grief attacks — those waves of loss that come crashing down, often unexpectedly — seemed to be triggered by things that were unusual, even weird. Jenny decided to share her observations with other grieving teens to validate that weird truly *is* normal when teenagers grieve.

Jenny lives in Naples, Florida, with her mom, their five rescued cats, two guinea pigs, and two pet frogs. She attends high

Jenny and her dad at Niagara Falls, just before he got sick

school at Seacrest School, where she enjoys cross country, track, and playing flute in the orchestra.

She also likes to write fiction, poems, and song lyrics; play electric guitar; travel; rollerblade; watch the Animal Planet and SyFy channels; and, of course, hang out with her friends.

Jenny is the author of *Lunch Box Love Notes from Dad* and the illustrator of two children's grief support books, *Timmy's Christmas Surprise* and *Heart-Shaped Pickles.*

How to ORder

Quality of Life Publishing Co. specializes in inspirational and gentle grief support books for readers of all ages. Here's how to order *Weird Is Normal When Teenagers Grieve* and other publications:

Bookstores: Available wherever books are sold

Online   www.QoLpublishing.com

Email: books@QoLpublishing.com

Phone: **1-877-513-0099**

                        Toll free in the U.S. and Canada

                        or call 1-239-513-9907 during regular

                        business hours, Eastern time.

Fax: **1-239-513-0088**

Mail: **Quality of Life Publishing Co.**

                        P.O. Box 112050

                        Naples, FL 34108-1929

Author Jenny Lee Wheeler speaks to groups of all sizes across North America. Call 1-877-513-0099 (toll free in the U.S. and Canada) to bring Jenny to your community.